# THE LEWIS AND CLARK EXPEDITION

A **TRUE BOOK**®

by

**Christin Ditchfield**

**Children's Press**®
A Division of Scholastic Inc.

New York  Toronto  London  Auckland  Sydney
Mexico City  New Delhi  Hong Kong
Danbury, Connecticut

A compass used by Lewis during the expedition

Content Consultant
**James D. Harlan**
Program Manager, Geographic
Resources Center, Department
of Geography, University
of Missouri

Reading Consultant
**Dr. Cecilia Minden-Cupp**
Former Director, Language
and Literacy Program
Harvard Graduate School
of Education

The illustration on the cover shows Sacagawea interpreting for the Lewis and Clark expedition. The photograph on the title page shows a dugout canoe on display at the Lewis and Clark National Historic Trail Interpretive Center in Montana.

Library of Congress Cataloging-in-Publication Data
Ditchfield, Christin.
    The Lewis and Clark Expedition / by Christin Ditchfield.
        p. cm. — (A True Book)
    Includes bibliographical references and index.
        ISBN 0-516-22835-8 (lib. bdg.)    0-516-25222-4 (pbk.)
        1. Lewis and Clark Expedition (1804–1806)—Juvenile literature.
2. West (U.S.)—Discovery and exploration—Juvenile literature. 3. West
(U.S.)—Description and travel—Juvenile literature. 4. Lewis, Meriwether,
1774–1809—Juvenile literature. 5. Clark, William, 1770–1838—Juvenile
literature. 6. Explorers—West (U.S.)—Biography—Juvenile literature.
I. Title. II. Series.
F592.7.D57 2006
917.804′2—dc22                                                         2005020413

CHILDREN'S PRESS, and A TRUE BOOK™, and associated logos are
trademarks and/or registered trademarks of Scholastic Library Publishing.
SCHOLASTIC and associated logos are trademarks and/or registered
trademarks of Scholastic Inc.
1 2 3 4 5 6 7 8 9 10 R 15 14 13 12 11 10 09 08 07 06

# Contents

In 1803, U.S. president Thomas Jefferson (above) wanted to buy some land from French emperor Napoléon Bonaparte (right).

# The Louisiana Purchase

In 1803, President Thomas Jefferson offered Napoléon Bonaparte, the emperor of France, two million dollars for the city of New Orleans. At that time, the Mississippi River marked the western border of the United States. Jefferson wanted to buy New Orleans and its seaport to help American merchants expand trade with Spain and France.

Napoléon told Jefferson that for fifteen million dollars he would sell him the entire Louisiana Territory. That land covered 820,000 square miles (2,123,800 square kilometers). The deal would double the size of the United States. The Louisiana Territory stretched from the Mississippi River all the way to the Rocky Mountains. It included all of what is now Louisiana,

A map of the
United States in 1803

Arkansas, Kansas, Oklahoma,
Missouri, Iowa, South Dakota, and
Nebraska, and parts of Colorado,
Minnesota, North Dakota,
Montana, Wyoming, and Texas.

Like many of the founders of the United States, Jefferson dreamed that the United States would one day stretch from coast to coast. The purchase of the Louisiana Territory would be a giant step toward making that dream come true. It would also give the United States a land route, and possibly a river route, to the Pacific Ocean. President Jefferson accepted Napoléon's offer. They named this agreement the Louisiana Purchase.

Thomas Jefferson signed the Louisiana Purchase papers in 1803.

# Preparing for Departure

No one knew for sure the exact size of the Louisiana Territory or what it contained. There were no reliable maps or charts. Few **explorers** had ever traveled so far west.

President Jefferson appointed his private secretary, Meriwether Lewis, to lead an **expedition**

A detail from a painted column in Astoria, Oregon, honors the Lewis and Clark expedition.

across the new U.S. territory. Lewis immediately asked his good friend William Clark to join him.

Some members of Lewis and Clark's crew were fur trappers.

The men pulled together a crew that, over time, numbered between forty and forty-six members. They chose people with the courage and skills to survive a long and difficult jour-ney. The crew included hunters, trappers, river men, and many soldiers from the U.S. Army, as well as Clark's African-American slave, York. Lewis brought along his dog, Seaman. The entire group formed the **Corps** of Discovery.

Meriwether Lewis (left)
and William Clark (right)
read books and studied
maps for their expedition.

To prepare for their expedition, Lewis and Clark studied
whatever information they
could find about the frontier.

Lewis made the travel arrangements. He purchased food, blankets, weapons, and other supplies. He bought a telescope

Meriwether Lewis used this telescope to learn about the stars. It is not clear if he took it on the expedition.

Lewis was in charge
of packing weapons,
camping supplies,
and medicine for
the trip.

and learned how to navigate
using the stars. Lewis asked doc-
tors to recommend medicines

and treatments for possible illnesses and injuries.

Lewis packed tools and ornaments to trade with the American Indians they would

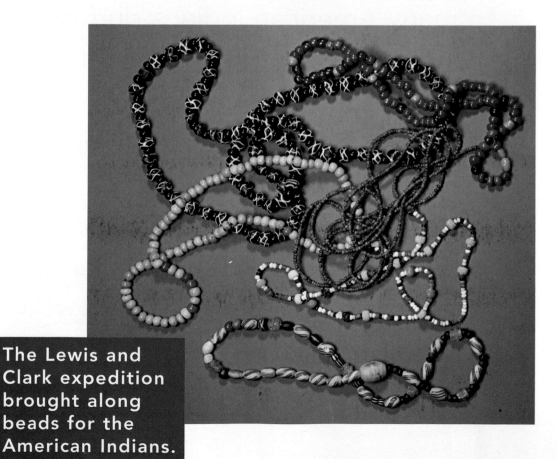

The Lewis and Clark expedition brought along beads for the American Indians.

meet along the way. The Indians would have animal skins, buffalo meat, and dried fish to trade. Clark had met many American Indians during his army days. He knew a lot about their traditions and beliefs. This knowledge turned out to be very valuable.

Most important, Lewis and Clark packed a supply of blank journals. They planned to fill them with detailed descriptions of the experience.

The men brought journals to record information. This journal belonged to William Clark.

They would keep a record of their expedition to share with others.

# A Dream Team

Lewis and Clark hunting bears in the forest

**M**eriwether Lewis met William Clark when they served in the army in 1795. Both men loved to hunt and hike and explore nature's wonders. The two adventurers soon became best friends. When their expedition began, Lewis was officially in charge. Yet he told the crew that he and Clark were cocaptains, with equal authority.

Lewis knew something about the study of plant and animal life, or biology. The crew respected him as a quiet, thoughtful leader. Clark was an expert mapmaker and navigator. His positive, cheerful energy kept spirits high during the journey. Together, Lewis and Clark made a terrific team.

A wall painting from the U.S. Capitol in Washington, D.C., showing Lewis and Clark watching an Indian village

# A Journey of Discovery

On May 14, 1804, Clark and the crew boarded a 55-foot (17-meter) boat and set sail from a camp near St. Louis on the Missouri River. Lewis joined the crew a few days later. Two smaller boats called **pirogues** carried the rest of the crew and the extra supplies.

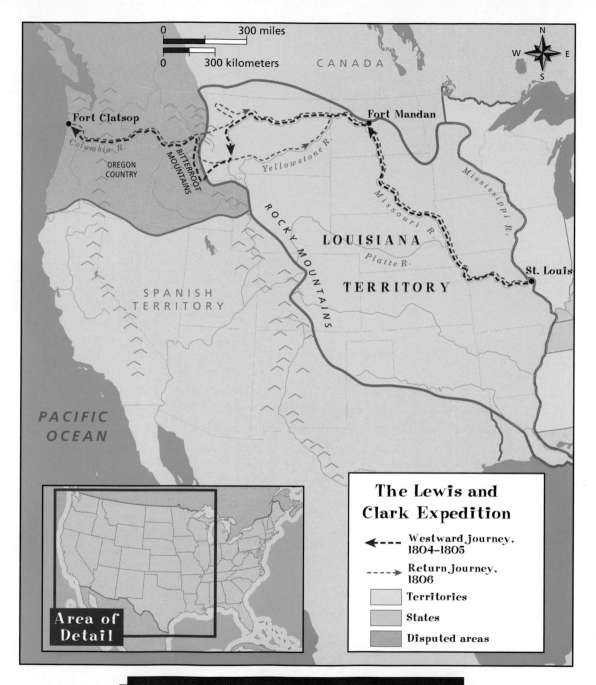

A map of the route followed by
the Lewis and Clark expedition

For much of their trip, Lewis and Clark traveled in dugout canoes called pirogues.

The explorers followed the westward course of the river. They traveled about 15 miles (24 km) a day. At night, they set up camp along the river.

Lewis and Clark found plenty to write about in their journals. They described each day's activities and accomplishments. Clark drew maps of the areas they explored. Both men included information on different types of rocks and **minerals,** plants, and trees.

In his journal, William Clark sketched an evergreen shrub leaf (top) and a California condor (bottom).

As they came to the Great Plains region, they found animals they had never seen before. They saw antelope, coyotes, prairie dogs, and grizzly bears.

Lewis kept a few of the smaller animals as pets. He sent others, including a black and white bird called a magpie, back home. He wanted President Jefferson to have some souvenirs of the expedition.

On the plains, the explorers encountered many different

American Indian tribes, including
the Omaha, Missouri, Teton,
Sioux, Mandan, Minnetaree, and
Shoshone. Lewis and Clark gave
the Indians gifts in exchange for
safe passage through their lands.

The Indians were often helpful to the crew. They gave them directions and suggested the best routes to travel. They also warned them of dangers ahead.

In April 1805, a French-Canadian fur trader named Toussaint Charbonneau joined the crew. He brought his Shoshone wife, Sacagawea, and their newborn son, Jean-Baptiste. Lewis and Clark were pleased to discover that Sacagawea knew the land well and could

Captain Meriwether Lewis meets the Shoshone.

help communicate with the other Indians. When it came time to cross the Rocky Mountains, Sacagawea traded with the Shoshone for horses.

# A Woman of Strength

**S**acagawea (pronounced SA-kag-uh-WEE-ah) is one of history's most famous American Indian women. In 1805, she served as a guide and translator for the Lewis and Clark expedition. With her infant son on her back, she helped lead the explorers Lewis and Clark through the wilderness, across North America. The explorers wrote in their journals that this Shoshone woman showed much courage and strength. They later said that they could not have made it without her.

A Sacagawea
U.S. dollar coin

The Corps of Discovery faced many difficulties on their journey. Sometimes their boats got stuck in shallow water. One almost sank during a storm. The summer heat made some men sick. Others became ill from traveling in the wind and rain. During a blizzard in the mountains, the crew ran out of food. They had to eat some of their horses to keep from starving to death.

Everyone got bitten by gnats, ticks, and mosquitoes. Several

This illustration by a crew member named Patrick Gass shows an overturned canoe during the journey.

men were attacked by grizzly bears. Lewis's dog once chased off a stampeding buffalo headed for the tent where Lewis and Clark were sleeping. Another time, some members of the

An expedition member fires at the Blackfoot Indians to protect the group's horses and supplies.

Blackfoot tribe tried to steal Lewis's horses and some supplies. It took great courage and determination for the Corps of Discovery to carry out its job.

# The Long Way Home

On November 18, 1805, Lewis and Clark climbed a mountain in Oregon and looked out to see the Pacific Ocean. They had made it all the way through the wilderness to the west coast.

Although they were disappointed not to have found a river route across the entire

Fort Clatsop, shown here as it looks today, was the expedition's winter camp.

country, they understood the importance of charting a land passage. They set up camp near what is now Astoria, Oregon, until the end of March 1806. They named their winter quarters Fort Clatsop.

The long journey home would be easier in some ways because they knew what to expect. However, there were still the same dangers and difficulties along the way.

After they crossed the Bitterroot Mountains, Lewis and Clark decided to split the crew in half and take different routes. They wanted to explore more before returning home. Clark led his group south along the Yellowstone River. Lewis led his group north, around the

Lewis and Clark reach the Missouri River.

Great Falls. They met up again at the Missouri River.

On September 23, 1806, Meriwether Lewis and William Clark arrived back in Saint Louis. Their incredible journey, a true success, had come to an end.

# A Welcome for Heroes

When the explorers finally returned home, they received a grand welcome. Parties and parades were held in their honor. Newspapers all over the country published accounts of their amazing expedition.

To thank Lewis and Clark for service to their country, the

U.S. government gave them each 1,600 acres (648 hectares) of the land they explored. Meriwether Lewis was appointed governor of the Louisiana Territory. William Clark was awarded the military rank of **brigadier general**. He was also named **superintendent** of Native Affairs. Clark continued to work closely with American Indians.

Lewis died mysteriously a few years after his return, in

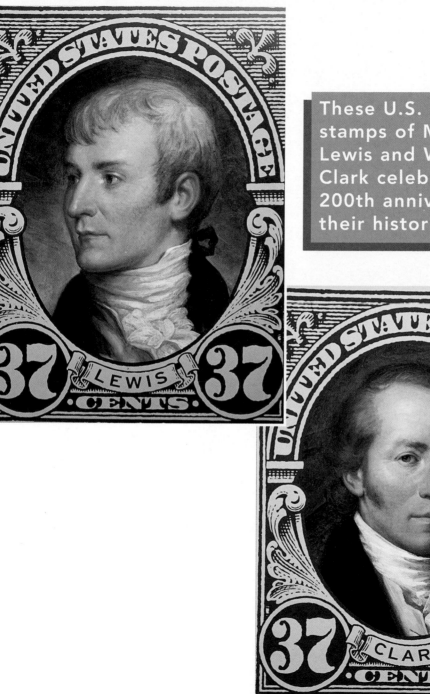

These U.S. postage stamps of Meriwether Lewis and William Clark celebrate the 200th anniversary of their historic trip.

1809. Clark died in 1838. For as long as they lived, Lewis and Clark cherished the memories of their historic expedition.

In two and a half years, Lewis and Clark traveled more than 8,000 miles (12,872 km). On their trip, the two leaders mapped mountains, rivers, and valleys. They identified hundreds of unknown plants and animals. They established peaceful relationships with more than fifty different

For Lewis and Clark, the expedition was always about the thrill of adventure and the excitement of discovery.

American Indian tribes. Above all, their efforts allowed those that followed to experience the wonders of the American West.

# To Find Out More

Here are some additional resources to help you learn more about the Lewis and Clark expedition:

 **Books**

Bursell, Susan. **Lewis and Clark Expedition.** Capstone Press, 2002.

Carter, E. J. **Lewis and Clark Journals.** Heinemann Library, 2003.

Herbert, Janis. **Lewis & Clark for Kids: Their Journey of Discovery with 21 Activities.** Chicago Review Press, Inc., 2000.

Lilly, Melinda. **Sacagawea, Lewis, and Clark.** Rourke Publishing, 2003.

Molzahn, Arlene Bourgeois. **Lewis & Clark: American Explorers.** Enslow Publishers, 2003.

Ransom, Candice F. **Lewis and Clark.** Lerner Publishing Group, 2003.

## Organizations and Online Sites

### Lewis and Clark: The Journey of the Corps of Discovery
*http://www.pbs.org/lewisandclark/*

Browse an archive of American Indian tribes that Lewis and Clark met on their journey. This site complements the film by Ken Burns.

### Lewis & Clark: Mapping the West
*http://www.edgate.com/lewisandclark/*

Look for information on the explorers and their expedition, interactive maps, and student learning activities.

### The Lewis and Clark Trail Heritage Foundation
6000 Central Avenue, Suite 327
Great Falls, MT 59403
406-454-1234
*http://www.lewisandclark.org*

This organization features information about the historic trail and an education page on its site.

### Lewis and Clark National Historic Trail
601 Riverfront Drive
Omaha, NE 68102
402-661-1804
*http://www.nps.gov/lecl/*

Find out about visiting portions of the original trail.

### National Museum of the American Indian
Fourth Street and Independence Avenue, S.W.
Washington, DC 20560
202-633-1000
*http://www.nmai.si.edu/*

Visit the first national museum dedicated to the life, languages, literature, history, and arts of the American Indians.

### Lewis and Clark Across Missouri
*http://lewisclark.geog.missouri.edu/index.shtml*

Check out interactive maps of the Lewis and Clark expedition, images of important river landmarks, and animated virtual Missouri River travel.

# Important Words

*brigadier general* a military rank between colonel and general

*corps* a group of people acting together for one purpose

*expedition* a long journey for a special purpose, such as exploring

*explorers* people who travel to learn more about unknown places

*minerals* things found in nature that are not animals or plants

*navigator* a person who uses maps, compasses, and other tools to travel

*pirogues* dugout canoes made from large logs

*superintendent* a manager of an organization

*translator* a person who speaks more than one language and helps others communicate

# Index

# Meet the Author

Christin Ditchfield is an accomplished educator, author, conference speaker, and host of the internationally syndicated radio program *Take It to Heart!* In addition to her books for parents and teachers, she has written more than forty books for children on a wide range of topics, including sports, science, history, literature, and civics. Ms. Ditchfield lives in Sarasota, Florida.